Retribution

Poems of the untold story of domestic abuse

Retribution

Poems of the untold story of domestic abuse

SARAH CARTER

Copyright © 2024 by Sarah Carter.

Published by Carter Publishing Ltd.

All rights reserved.

No part of this publication may be reproduced, distributed, or transmitted in any form or by any means, including photocopying, recording, or other electronic or mechanical methods, without the prior written permission of the publisher, except as permitted by U.K. copyright law.

For permission requests, contact:

www.carter-publishing.com

enquiries@carter-publishing.com

The views and opinions expressed in these poems are not based on or relate to any one individual or organisation.

ISBN: 978-1-0685204-0-2 (print)

ISBN: 978-1-0685204-1-9 (E-book)

This book of poems is about domestic abuse, but not as you've read it before.

I'm done looking inward and taking the blame. And I'm done with all the lies and the shame.

So, this book is about domestic abuse, but not as you've read it before.

It's about how society views domestic abuse. With all its hypocrisy, double standards and excuse after excuse.

It's full of anger and rage, hurt and dismay.

It's a shout for action, it's a call for change.

So, join me if you may, to rant and rave. Let's vent together, and then maybe, one day things will change.

From a survivor

For survivors

Contents

You are as guilty as I 12

They call me a victim 18

The successful psychopath 22

You're free 28

I want change 32

They talk 36

You need to be a victim 40

I'm fooling myself 44

The Monsters are real 50

Denial runs both ways 58

Why is it my fault? 66

They go on 70

Not a real victim 74

Prejudice 80

I will never be free 84

Survivors 90

Justice 96

Author's Note

Acknowledgements

About the author

You are as guilty as I

Why did you stay?
The loaded question that is asked so quickly.

Yet you are just as guilty as I am.

Blind to the person right in front of you.
Their charm and charisma make it
so easy to forget.
So easy to believe their truth.

But you are just as guilty as I.

I saw what was behind closed doors,
you didn't even see the door.

I screamed the truth when I saw it,
but you chose to ignore it.

I shouted and pleaded
but you just turned away.

Yet you point the finger at me,
asking why did I stay?

When you are as guilty as I.

It took some time but now
my eyes are wide open.

You had just as much time, but your eyes
are bound shut.

Why? You question,
like I am to blame.

Why? I question,

are you still looking the wrong way.

The truth eludes you,

just as it did I.

Yet you think yourself innocent,

not complicit in their crime.

How? I wonder, can you not see.

Yet I am the one branded blind and weak.

Denial they say.

Denial I say.

For you are as vulnerable as I.

Denial won't protect you,

just as it didn't protect me.

They'll come for you

as they came for me.

Denial they say with pity in their gaze.

Denial I say won't protect you from the

monsters in the day.

They call me a victim

They call me a victim,
but that seems so wrong and strange.

I was always so strong,
how could all of that have changed?

They call me a victim,
like I was helpless and afraid.

But I fought back, I stood up,
I shouted out their name.

They call me a victim,
then turn their back and walk away.

Like nothing can be done,
like nothing can be changed.

They call me a victim,
it's not my actual name.

But that's who I am now,
just a number and not a name.

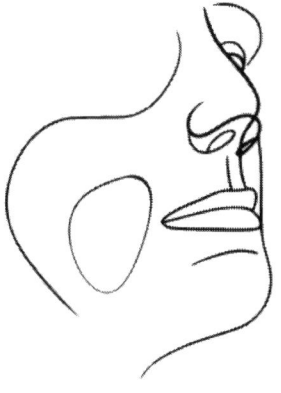

The successful psychopath

The successful psychopath.
Have you heard of them?
They're a predator, they're a myth.

Some scientists even claim that they might not exist.

They look the same as you or I.
Forming part of the high-street, forming part of the sky.

They could be a cook,
a dentist, a florist, or a cop.
Hiding in plain sight,
always watching, always hot.

A serial killer they may not be.
But don't be fooled,
don't invite them for tea.

Just one moment, that's all they need.
To seduce, to charm, to completely disarm.

The successful psychopath.
Have you heard of them?
They're a predator, they're a myth.

But they'll deny it, if you mention that
they exist.

Always lurking in the shadows,
careful not to leave a mark.
They'll hurt you in ways you can't imagine
and then go back into the dark.

You can scream and shout,
but it will make no difference.
They will just stand there in complete
indifference.

You can go to the police,
but the answer will be the same.
You made it all up, how could they?
Now, just go away.

The successful psychopath.
Have you heard of them?
They're a predator, they're a myth.

They're everywhere yet nowhere,
while society denies they exist.

But you know the truth, just as I do,
that they exist.

They are clever, agile, remorseless
and absolute.

They will control every narrative and twist
every truth.

But they can't hide forever,
for we know who they are.

Their cloak of darkness and denial will only
protect them for a while.

And when the light comes,
as surely it will.

Their schemes will go up in flames,
as they burn in the sun.

You're free

You're free they say,
like everything is just fine.

Like the threats have all stopped.
Like everything is sunshine.

But you're free, they say,
wondering why I'm so scared.

Not seeing what's still there.
Not seeing how nothing's changed.

But you're free they say,
getting angry and impatient.

Not understanding what's at play.
Not understanding how it
hasn't all gone away.

But you're free they say,
getting bored and moving on.

Like I am the problem.
Like I won't just move on.

But I'm not free I say,
getting scared and upset.

Screaming how nothing has changed.
How it hasn't all gone away.

But you're free they say.

I want change

I want accountability.

I want change.

I want to scream in their face.

I want to light it all up.

I want to burn down this place.

I want justice.

I want change.

I want to run the other way.

I want to rip it all down.

I want to rebuild a new way.

I want revenge.

I want change.

I want to wish it all away.

I want to start the last fight.

I want to end it all right.

They talk

They talk and talk and talk and talk and talk
and talk and talk and talk and talk and talk.

Until you say STOP!

Then they talk and talk and talk and talk and
talk and talk and talk and talk and talk and
talk and talk.

You need to be a victim

You need to be a victim
and a victim is weak and small.

It's the only way it makes sense.
It's the only way to conform.

But what if you're not a typical victim,
not weak and small?

What if you're a different victim
that is strong and tall?

Then you are not a victim.
You do not match or conform.

Victims who are strong and tall
make no sense at all.

There is no other way.

You need to be a victim,
and victims are weak and small.

I'm fooling myself

I hope things will change,
but I'm fooling myself.

They pretend to try.
Talking the talk and changing the law.

But nothing has changed.

Coercive control is a crime now,
yet it's a crime that no one commits.
Or is it just a crime that no one admits?

Sometimes it looks like change,
but I'm fooling myself.

Society doesn't care about
abuse and karma.

They just want to sit there,
watching the hate and drama.

So, nothing will change.

I fight for change,
but I'm fooling myself.

The police have more power now,
but they refuse to use it.

Why should I be surprised when they
are the ones behind it.

How silly was I to expect
anything to change.

To think that justice and safety
would ever come our way.

I need to stop fooling myself
and admit the truth.

A society founded by abuse will never
protect from abuse.

The Monsters are real

The world is different now.

The monsters are real.

It looks the same as it did before,
but life will never be the same now I've
seen through that door.

Yet somehow, no one else seems to know
that the monsters are real.

Instead, they question the way I feel.

Like I am seeing things,
that I am crazy and unstable.

While I sit there fearing they
are just unable.

For I know the truth now – the monsters
are real.

They've been there all along,
not even trying to hide it.

Yet nobody sees them,
while they disguise it.

For they are smiling and charming
not vulgar and alarming.

The perfect person to all who don't know.

Until you close the door,
and the truth starts to show.

Sirens, vampires, psychopaths and more.

They've had many names over the years,
yet they allude them once more.

For myths and tales are but make believe.
Not a real threat to how we breathe.

Denial keeps them safe,
or so they think.

Until it's their blood that
they want to drink.

Then they'll see the truth,
if they survive of course.

That the person in front of them
truly has no remorse.

And they can cry and scream for
justice and admission.

But it will make no difference
while nobody will listen.

We try to take solace thinking, at least now
they know - that the monsters are real.

But that doesn't change how
the world now feels.

Them seeing the truth doesn't
change the truth.

And them screaming in their face doesn't
make us anymore safe.

For they are one of us now.

Tainted like us now.

Not believed liked us now.

Ignored liked us now.

Denial runs both ways

In the relationship they told me
to leave, like it was the most obvious
thing in the world.

Accepting any other outcome
was utterly absurd.

Protect your children they would say.
Noting the chaos and disarray.

Highlighting the hurt and the danger,
like my children would be safer with
a stranger.

And if I doubted or protested,
they would question my judgement.

Saying I'm blind with denial,
to think their actions as anything
other than vile.

But what they don't see,
is denial runs both ways.

And the truth they speak now
doesn't go all the way.

For when it comes down to it,
with the courts and services.

Showing anything other than love
only makes them nervous.

You must promote the
relationship they say,
ignoring the violence
and disarray.

Because they don't want to believe
the fear and the danger.

Instead, they choose to brand
me a liar and a hater.

Oblivious to the mirror that they hold,
the double standards and truths untold.

Favouring the fantasy world of denial,
where everything will be fine
after such a short while.

And if you dare to challenge their thinking,
they will put you in a hole that you will
surely sink in.

Parent alienation is their favourite
false allegation.

Stopping you in your tracks under
threat of attack.

And all I want is for them to see the truth,
to protect my children from the dangers
under that roof.

But what was once told has all gone away,
now I'm the ex and not the current
one in play.

For they never truly understood,
the real dangers in the woods.

That the violence and disarray were
only part of the display.

For the truth is much deeper,
darker and sinister.

A scary land to be,

so, they choose not to see.

Not realising that they are

acting just like me.

Why is it my fault?

Victims should do more to protect themselves.

Dress the right way, socialise the right way, walk the right way and talk the right way.

But why is it my fault?

Victims should stand up for themselves.

Scream at the sight of danger, run and not go home with a stranger.

But why is it my fault?

Victims should educate themselves.

Set firmer boundaries, spot the signs sooner and look for a better suitor.

But why is it my fault?

I didn't stalk, harass and obsess and I didn't attack, manipulate and cause distress.

So why is it my fault?

They go on

They go on and on and on and on and on
and on and on and on and on and on.

Until you shout ENOUGH!

Then they go on and on and on and on and
on and on and on and on and on.

Not a real victim

People who are real victims have no
control to stop the crime.

Unlike you, who could have
left at any time.

You're not scared and you're
not held hostage.

Instead, you're just sat there whining
that you were accosted.

Can't you just sort yourself out and find
something else to whine about?

You're wasting everyone's time with
your hate and your lies.

Don't you know I have real
criminals to find.

It's just a domestic it's not
our problem.

So, I'll be on my way now,
unless you have a real problem?

Don't you realise,
I am a real victim.

I couldn't make it stop and
I couldn't just leave.

They would hunt me down and
make me bleed.

I am scared and I am
held hostage.

They'll destroy my life if you
don't stop them!

Can't you stop complaining,
and actually put the work in?

I'm not wasting your time,
I'm reporting a crime!

They are a real criminal,
and what they did was more
than out of line.

It's not just a domestic and it is

your problem.

Stop walking away so you can

ignore it another day.

You need to do a lot more,

like uphold the law!

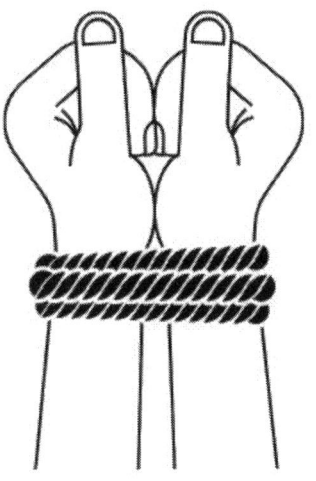

Prejudice

There's supposed to be no prejudice in law,

but everywhere you turn there's

prejudice at the door.

The police, the court, your counsel

and your support.

They all have an opinion that they

want to report.

Shaped by years of repression and

oppression.

They see nothing more than love

and aggression.

But like narcissistic lies,
the truth holds no place.

And the love that they see is
in the opposite place.

So, when you ask them to protect,
all you get is neglect.

And a prejudice that holds a
knife to your neck.

I will never be free

I will never be free,
not while their tied to me.

But that is something that
you will never see.

You say that I'm free,
telling me to move on and be me.

And I try and I try,
but it will never come to be.

For that link will always
hold them to me.

And I love that link
for all who they are.

The light in the dark.
The flower from the thorn.

Yet they're also the link
who ties them to me.

The reason I will never be free.

The continuation is a special form of hell.
Full of worry, excuses, and the hope that all
will be well.

So I say I'm worried,
and you tell me they have changed.

Yet, when I wanted to stay,
You said it will always be that way.

So what is the difference?

The link is the difference.

But the difference is in what you say,
and not what they do.

So I become a shield,
to protect from what will always be.

Protecting from what I'm
trying to escape.

Free, yet not free.

Not while they're tied to me.

Survivors

We stick together us survivors. For we are
the only ones who truly understand.

We don't question why, because we know
why, and we don't turn away because we
have the courage to stay.

You'll never hear us say 'but they didn't look
abusive', because we know that their look
could always be illusive.

We'll compare notes and laugh
at their bad 'jokes'.

Predicting their staged response and
knowing it wasn't just used once.

We take comfort seeing how
they are all the same.

Using their age-old lines,
guilt trips and manipulative ways.

We know nothing will be done,
as we all line up one by one.

But we can be there for each other.
Knowing what we do, like no other.

So, we stick together us survivors.
For we are all we have.

We make each other stronger and fight so
that it won't last much longer.

We provide an ear to vent and a shoulder to
cry on. Supporting each other as we go, like
a life raft to ride on.

We watch out for newcomers and warn
those that we know. Hoping beyond hope
that Clare's Law will show.

But the fight is endless,
and the war is far from won.

Everyday a thousand fall,
with consequence to none.

All the while society keeps on churning,
with not even a glimmer that things are
turning.

Denial and confusion scare them all away.
Instead, they just ask 'why did you stay?'

That's why we stick together us survivors.
For we are the only ones who truly
understand.

The only ones that 'get it',
The only ones we have.

Justice

I dream of a way it could be,
where justice would be served,
and people would be free.

It is a land devoid of victim blaming,
excuses and drama.

Instead, there would be understanding,
knowledge and karma.

There would be a day to remember all
those who didn't make it.

And effective protection for those who
are still trying to escape it.

There would be empathy in the courts,
and police who support.

Cafcass would be scrapped,
and the bias would be axed.

There would be no more prejudice
and discrimination.

Instead, there would be evidence
and investigation.

The research would be updated,
and our children would be protected.

And if they step out of line
there will be an ombudsman,
to remind.

Conversations will change and people
won't look the other way,
or ask why did you stay?

Instead, they will listen and understand,
realising that things were never that bland.

They won't jump to conclusion or
run with assumptions.

And they will see that parental alienation,
was a matter of protection,
and not a lack of connection.

The media will play their part,
knowing that click bait is not art.

And the government will stand up and
take true responsibility.

Rather than hiding behind charities to
avoid accountability.

There will be a register of offenders,
and extra consequences for serial offences.

It will be a matter for the state,
a problem for all.

There will be no more hiding
behind closed doors.

It will take a while to change,
as people slowly adjust.

But things will be made easier with
a system they can trust.

But alas, this is a land of make believe,

and in reality,

people are far from free.

But that doesn't stop me dreaming

of how it might be.

In a land where justice would be served,

and people would be free.

"I alone cannot change the world, but I can cast a stone across the waters to create many ripples."

- Mother Teresa

Author's Note

I never thought that I would be a poet. In fact, in all honesty, the prospect was truly laughable.

As a kid with severe dyslexia the prospect of achieving any literary goal seemed completely out of reach to me. And I was okay with that *(yes, I did just start a sentence with a joining word).* But as I grew older and started my tertiary education, I found a fondness for writing and a style that people found engaging *(I know, I did it again).*

Yet, the idea of being a poet was still so far from my radar that it might as well not have existed. Until one night, inspiration struck.

It was never meant to be a poem. It was supposed to be the bones of a closing statement for a book, but by the time I'd finished it, it was most certainly a poem – *You are as guilty as I.*

Not wanting to let the poem go to waste I decided to write more poems to create this book – another laughable prospect. But I gave it a go and I like to think that it has turned out quite well.

And here I am, a poet by accident, but a poet none the less.

So, to the dyslexic kids out there - Don't let a label like 'dyslexia' hold you back. If you want to write, follow your dreams and write.

Now, don't get me wrong, spell check and Grammarly will be your lifeline, and definitely invest in a proofreader! But so what? Every other author uses them anyway. They just see less red squiggly lines than us, that's all.

Acknowledgements

This book has been surprisingly therapeutic to write and came at a time when I really needed a distraction.

Through writing it, I feel less powerless as I add a voice to the fight, and I hope reading it has brought you similar comfort.

I would like to thank everyone who has helped make this book a reality. I couldn't have done it without your support.

I would like to thank my Mum for being a wonderful proofreader as always.

And I would like to thank my good friend Jennifer for getting so excited about this project. Your belief in me really helped me push through the final stages of making this book a reality.

I would thank society for providing the inspiration for this book but that doesn't really seem right. The systems within our society have failed me and my children time and time again, and I am certainly not thankful for it. But I suppose making money from this book is a small consolation.

About the author

Sarah Carter is a British author, poet, activist and mother. She is also a survivor.

Sarah was in an abusive relationship for nine years and has experienced the perils of family court and the police.

Since the end of her relationship, she has dedicated her life to helping other survivors heal from the impact of domestic abuse, with a particular focus on psychological abuse.

She has fought for survivors right to justice and campaigned MPs and the police with her research.

This is her first poetry book aimed at highlighting society's contribution to domestic abuse.

I hope you enjoyed this book of poems. If you would like to read more of my work, check out my website or follow along on social media.

www.carter-publishing.com

@SCarterPub

Carter Publishing Ltd

Printed in Great Britain
by Amazon